Pl IN

Daisy Neal

To: Merrilyn.

"The hand of our God is upon all them for good that seek Him." Ezra. 8.22.

With my love to you.

Auntie Daisy.

14th February 1992

ARTHUR H. STOCKWELL LTD.
Elms Court Ilfracombe Devon
Established 1898

First published in Great Britain, 1991

By the same author:
Poems of Praise and Promise

ISBN 0 7223 2589-4

Printed in Great Britain by
Arthur H. Stockwell Ltd.
Elms Court Ilfracombe
Devon

Dedicated to:
My dear friends Elfryn and Iris Matthews,
with my grateful thanks
for their interest and encouragement in my writing.

THE LORD SHALL SUSTAIN THEE Ps. 55 22

THE SNOWDROP

The month of February brings
  Bitter wind which bites and stings;
With snow to block the lane
  And cold, driving rain —
The bleakest month of all the year.
  But with it comes, our hearts to cheer
The small snowdrop, with tiny flower
  Like a pure white bell,
Nodding in wind and rain, to tell
  Of soon coming Spring.

Oh! you sweet and shy white flower,
  Through snow and wind and shower,
Though February's chill wind sting
  Such joy to all our hearts you bring,
For we know that He Who made you
  And sustains you,
Will sustain us too,
  When in life's wintry blasts we're tossed,
Feeling that we're almost lost;
  Safely through the Lord will bring us
By His grace
  To see the sunshine of His face.

LORD. THOU KNOWEST THAT I LOVE THEE John 21 17

Do you ever
  Try to measure
Jesus' love for you?
  Sometimes I do.
But when I think of all the story,
How he left Heaven's glory
  To die on Calvary's tree
      For me —
      I pause —
      Because —
    I have no word
    That I can say,
      Except —
    I love You Lord.

THE SPIRIT OF TRUTH . . . . . SHALL TAKE OF MINE AND SHOW IT UNTO YOU   John 16   13 & 15

When Springtime morning mists display
  An opalescent, milky ray;
And from the misty morns of May
  Steals out the pearly dawn of day.
It is an awe-inspiring thing
  To realise the sheen of Spring
Again upon the hedgerows seen
  In soft delicate shades of green.
When tree buds open in a slow
  And multi-coloured, opaque glow.

But the mysterious, shadowy sheens
  Will soon give place to vivid greens,
As though upon the Springtime blush
  Thin coats of varnish, with a brush,
By unseen hands have been painted
  That we all may be acquainted
With a brighter, deeper sheen,
  Which by wondering eyes is seen —
Nature's full glory come to birth.

This gentle opening, hour by hour,
  Is as the soul's awakening
By the Holy Spirit's power;
  When sin-dimmed eyes are cleared to see
The wonder and the mystery,
  Of the Saviour's matchless love,
That He should leave His home above,
  To give His life at Calvary
For sinners, such as you and me.

HE CAME UNTO HIS OWN, AND HIS OWN RECEIVED HIM NOT. BUT AS MANY AS RECEIVED HIM, TO THEM GAVE HE POWER TO BECOME THE SONS OF GOD
John 1 11, 12

Leaving His Father's side,
  He came from Heaven alone,
To be identified
  With those who would not own
Kinship with Him.
  His glorious High Throne
Which was from the beginning
  Empty He left,
To dwell unrecognised, unknown
  By those He called His Own.
But eyes of strangers saw His glory,
  In adoration bowed before Him;
Kneeled before Him in glad worship
  Owning His eternal Kingship.
And to these, though not His Kinsmen
  Power He gave, His sons to be;
Born into His family
  By Heavenly mystery.

WE LOVE HIM BECAUSE HE FIRST LOVED US
1 John 4 19

Silently the snow has fallen
From Heaven above to Earth below;
Silently the flowers are pushing
Upwards, through the earth and snow.

Birds now silent soon will sing
In joyous trill, to greet the Spring;
May your heart be joyful too
In loving Him who first loved you.

LO! I AM WITH YOU ALWAY   Matt. 28   20

The Saviour understands
  All your sorrow.
Holds out His hands
  Says "Come to Me
Dread not the morrow.
  Fear not the dark
Of days you cannot see,
  For I am with you
And your strength and light
  Will ever be,
Now, and through eternity."

POUR OUT YOUR HEART BEFORE HIM   Psalm 62   8

He loves to hear His children call,
  Pour out your heart before Him.
Be your sorrow great or small,
  Caused by grief or caused by sin.
Pour out your heart before Him
  TELL HIM ALL.

He longs to bear your heavy load,
  Pour out your heart before Him.
Be your burden sin or sorrow
  Leave it not until tomorrow,
NOW pour out your heart before Him
  TELL HIM ALL.

All your sin He bore at Calvary,
  Pour out your heart before Him.
He'll forgive and make you whole,
  In the turmoil of your soul
Pour out your heart before Him
  TELL HIM ALL.

He shed His blood to give you peace,
  Pour out your heart before Him.
To give you joy and sweet release
  From every sorrow every sin.
Pour out your heart before Him
  TELL HIM ALL.

Oh! What an invitation!
  Oh! What a loving Saviour!
Who could be a Friend so tender?
  Who so patiently will listen?
As pouring out your heart before Him
  YOU TELL HIM ALL.

HE WAS THERE IN THE WILDERNESS – AND WAS WITH THE WILD BEASTS *Mark 1 13*

He, the Lord of Earth and Heaven,
Into the wilderness was driven
By the Spirit's activation
To be tempted of the Devil.
Striving against the elements,
Of strength drained, weary and alone.
To the earth He sank
Calling in faltering tone
Upon His Father.
The ever-watchful, prowling beasts
Hearing His sad cry,
Encircled Him to spy
Who dare invade their territory.
Silent language passed between them
"This is no mortal man we see.
He is the Lord of Earth and Heaven
Encircle and protect Him."
Hyena, wolf, lion, bear
In close proximity draw near.
Behind Him the lion his body stretched,
And on his mane the Great Creator slept.
Only the sound of soft breathing
Falls on the silent night,
And warmed by the breath of beasts
The Great Creator sleeps,
Until with coming morning light
Silently steal the beasts away
And returns the Devil to the affray.

Forty nights the beasts thus guard
In sleep, their Heavenly Lord.
But mortal man for whom He came to die
Could not one hour of vigil with Him keep
When He, exhausted by agony of death impending,
Longed for the solace of their company.

Oh! Lord, forgive us all that we
Spend so little time with Thee.
Teach us how to set apart
Time that will rejoice Thy heart.
And thus the promise of Thy Word
Fulfilled will be –
"Draw near to God, and He
Will draw near to Thee."

HE TOOK A TOWEL AND GIRDED HIMSELF . . . . . AND BEGAN TO WASH THE DISCIPLES' FEET *John 13 5, 6*

The Great Creator, Lord of Heaven,
  Sustainer of the Universe,
Stoops at His disciples' feet.
  In His hands a bowl of water,
Round His waist a towel girt;
  And each dirt-stained, roughened foot
Into His gentle hands He takes,
  Washing them with loving care.
Loosens the towel for to dry them
  While the men around Him stare,
Noting each loving action, mute,
  Dumbed by service so majestic;
Drained of courage, none dared ask Him
  Why He served as servant lowly,
He, the Son of God most Holy.
  Comes He now to Peter's seat,
Lays down the bowl at his feet.
  But Peter draws away and cries,
"Lord, Thou shalt never wash my feet."
  Sadly the Saviour then replies,
"If this service I do not for thee,
  Then Peter thou hast no part with Me."
With passion Peter loudly cries,
  "My hands Lord then, and my head too
For I must have my part with You,
  My God, my Saviour and my Lord."

Lord, may we this lesson learn,
  "By love serve one another"
And give us, by the Spirit's grace
  Power to take the lowest place,
Clothed in His humility,
  That all around may clearly see
Our love for Him and one another.

NOW IS THE DAY OF SALVATION *2 Corinth. 6 2*

Above the little rippling stream
  Between green, grassy banks,
Runs a narrow winding path
  Shaded by may trees, oak and ash;
Then over a little wooden bridge
  Where 'twixt the slats is clearly seen
The busy little rippling stream.
  But sunlight does not glow
On the bridge or stream below,
  For standing by protectively
Spreading long and massive arms
  Is a great horse-chestnut tree,
Sheltering the bridge and stream, and all
  Who cross the little wooden bridge
To a gate in a great stone wall.

From morning through afternoon
  The gate stands open wide,
And all who will may pass through
  A garden with lawns and flowers,
To the highway on the far side,
  And gaze as they go at the old stone house,
And in a far corner view
  The gnarled trunk of an ancient yew
Where soft-eyed ring doves bill and coo
  In the lazy days of summer.

But each day at five of the clock
  Comes a man with a key to lock
The gate in the great stone wall;
  Then alas! alas! for all
Who comes to pass through the gate
  To the highway which lies beyond
For it is, Too late! Too late!
  For now securely locked is the gate.

As I think of the little winding path
  I remember one also, narrow and straight
Leading right up to Heaven's gate,
  Where Jesus our Saviour waits, and receives
Each sinner who comes and on Him believes,
  Saying, "Welcome to My Father's Home
And the place prepared for you alone."
  But that gate will not always open be,
One day it will close for eternity;
  Then a cry will go up, "Too late! Too late!
Closed for ever is Heaven's gate."

THE PATH OF THE JUST IS AS THE SHINING LIGHT, THAT SHINETH MORE AND MORE UNTO THE PERFECT DAY *Prov. 4 18*

Between high banks it ripples,
  The little winding stream;
But the sunshine does not reach it,
  Not a single gleam,
For along the banks are standing
  Trees, both strong and tall
Whose branches stretch and intertwine,
  Hiding the rays of bright sunshine,
From the little rippling stream.
  Does then the little stream not flow
Because it sees no sunshine glow?
  Oh! no. Oh! no. Still on it goes
Then into bright sunlight it flows
  Sparkling, dazzling, rippling gaily,
Flowing, tinkling, hourly, daily.

Thus may we in days of darkness
  Still happily pursue our way,
Holding to God's faithful promise
  That there is a perfect day
Soon to dawn for all His children,
  Where the Lord Himself shall be
Their sun and light eternally.

THY HAND SHALL LEAD ME, AND THY RIGHT HAND SHALL HOLD ME UP   Psalm 139   10

Ferociously the March wind blows
  And the tall, tall coniferous trees
Toss and rear and twirl
  Round and around about.
But atop the highest bough
  Perches a starling, clinging tight,
Swirling and turning without fright.
  What mighty strength is in his claws
That with such fierce tenacity
  He holds the tossing, rearing bough.
He does not fear to crash below,
  For his claws will not let him go
Until he lifts his wings
  And soars above upon the winds.

Lord, we may not keep our grasp of Thee,
  When in sorrow or perplexity;
So, when present circumstance bewilder
  Be Thou, Holy Spirit our Reminder
Of our Father's faithful Word,
  That wherever we may be
This is the promise of the Lord,
  "With MY Hand I will lead thee
And My right Hand shall hold thee up."

THE FOOL HATH SAID IN HIS HEART, "THERE IS NO GOD" Psalm 14 1

What colour could the grass have been
  If not green?
And what the sky's hue
  If not blue?
How long day and night
  If you think the hours not right?
You say some birds are wingless born
  But for convenience to obtain
Their daily food, wings they grew.
  So man, as you so long to fly
Why have not wings evolved for you?
  You say, some creatures, at will
Have changed their shape to fit the bill,
  Then why are you, as man intelligent
In such matters negligent?

Man you are, and full of knowledge,
  Then tell me how a little crocus
With the urge of life in Spring,
  Will perform a mighty feat
By pushing up through hard concrete,
  To open petals like a goblet,
And drink in the bright sunlight?

These things mentioned here to you.
  Are but a very, very few
Of the wonders of creation.
  Surely then such arrogance as yours
To say, "There is no God",
  Is really crass stupidity,
When all can see God's perfect laws
  Working without diversion
Throughout the whole creation,
  As in the sun and moon and stars,
With perfect accuracy.

Oh! bow down before Him now,
  While opportunity allow.
Own Him, the Great Creator,
  King of Kings and Lord of Lords.
For the day is coming soon
  When to Him all knees must bow,
And every tongue confess
  That He, Who made the Universe
And all that is therein,
  Is the King of all creation
God, and Lord of every nation.

HE HATH BORNE OUR GRIEFS
AND CARRIED OUR SORROWS *Isaiah 53 4*

Who like the Man of Sorrows
  Knows your sorrow?
Who understands your grief
  Like Him with grief acquainted?
Who can bear your burdens
  Like Christ the crucified?
But He is risen and alive
  And gently bids you,
"Come to Me, and rest."

HE WAS WOUNDED FOR OUR TRANSGRESSIONS, AND BRUISED FOR OUR INIQUITIES *Isaiah 53 5*

See the suffering Saviour dying
On the cross at Calvary.
In His agony despised,
In His suffering rejected.
Bearing in His body
All our sin.

Pressed upon His sweating brow,
Crown of sharpest thorn.
Rent His side by piercing sword,
Hands and feet by great nails torn.
Suffering Saviour, bleeding, dying
For our sin.

Buried, but triumphant rose,
Mighty Victor o'er His foes.
Sin and death He has defeated,
Now beside His Father seated,
Blessed Lamb of Calvary –
Praying for us.

COME YE YOURSELVES APART . . . . .
AND REST AWHILE Mark 6 31

Are the burdens of the day
  Too heavy?
Do the trials of your way
  Press you down?
Do your loved ones cause you grief
  And you cannot find relief
From your sorrow?
  Listen! Listen!
Quietly listen.
  Hear the Saviour speaking;
Pause and listen to His voice.
  "Come, my child and rest awhile
With Me apart.
  All your sorrows I have carried,
All your burdens I have borne.
  Do not let your mind be harried
Nor your spirit torn.
  Come, and rest with Me apart,
I'll bid your sorrows all depart
  And My peace in all its fulness,
Fill your heart with quietness
  Which the world can never give
Nor can take away.
  Come. Come with Me apart
Rest awhile."

THE LIGHT OF THE KNOWLEDGE OF THE GLORY OF GOD IN THE FACE OF JESUS CHRIST *2 Cor. 4 6*

Oh! What beauty is revealed
  By the evening sun in Spring,
As it sheds its rosy beam
  Upon the tree trunks,
And reveals the tiny, opening leaf buds,
  Silhouetted against blue sky
Pale pink tinted.

This rosy glow o'er Nature spread
  Is as the hallowed light,
Which beams from those whose sight
  Is ever fixed upon the Saviour's face,
With all the beauty of its heavenly grace.
  From which reflects
The light of knowledge
  Of God's glory.

Oh! Lord keep our eyes
  Upon Thy face,
That the light of Thine Own grace
  In us be seen.
Though we, unconscious of the ray
  May, day by day
Reflect Thy glory.

THE LORD IS GOOD TO ALL: AND HIS TENDER MERCIES ARE OVER ALL HIS WORKS *Psalm 145 9*

As currants spread within a cake,
  Birds on bare branches perch
On cold and misty days,
  In bleakest winter time.
With backs humped
  And feathers ruffled,
Miserable and troubled
  Through scarcity of food,
Casting swift glances round
  Lest any morsel on the ground
They overlook.
  The black, bare branches sway
In winter wind in the misty day.
  But the black, feathery balls remain
Upon the black, bare branches,
  Warmth and energy to retain
That swift may be the downward flight
  When each pair of bright eyes sight
A likely titbit.

But betwixt the raw, cold days
  Come some that are most pleasant;
And when the sunshine calls
  Those huddled, feathery balls
Return to their slim lines
  Cheeping with joyous notes
Searching hedgerows with the hopes
  To find some insect or an early bud.
Then at last comes Spring,
  When each erstwhile feathery ball
Stands slim and tall
  To sing and sing and sing.

Oh! Lord may we as patient be
  As all Thy feathered family,
For whom Thou carest.
  When we pass through cold, dark days
Help us still to give Thee praise;
  Because we know Thy Word is sure
And for ever will endure,
  "The Lord is good to all
And tender are His mercies
  Over all His works."

THE LORD SHALL REJOICE IN HIS WORKS
Psalm 104 31

What volume of traffic in the air
  In Springtime!
When happy birds each build a nest,
  Speeding swiftly east and west —
They know whither.
  Each one carrying in his beak
Stick, straw or feather.

Some dart like arrow from a bow,
  Some fly with floppy flight — as crow,
But in the mode of scallop, flit
  The family of the wee blue tit,
Up and down, up and down.
  Swiftly darts the sleek magpie
To the ring-dove's nest, to spy
  If she has her first eggs laid;
Then makes a sudden, vicious raid
  To steal one of the clutch, for food
For his ever-hungry brood.

From hour to hour the traffic plies
  Of feathered bodies, with bright eyes,
All aquiver with excitement
  As they work for the achievement
Of a warm and sheltered nest
  Where their little ones can rest.

But with all this rushing traffic,
  Backwards and forwards in the air,
There are no mid-air collisions
  To cause calamity or stir
Between the hurrying, busy builders.
  No need for traffic-lights, or beacons,
For these flying, feathered bodies
  Work by God's remote control;
He, their Maker and their Lord
  Loves the whole of His creation
And He guides them by His Word.

MY PRAYER FOR YOU

For you I pray,
  The Lord bless you.
Reveal to you His way
  Every day.
Strengthen you in weakness
  By His power.
With the fulness of His joy
  Fill you,
That you may sing His praise
  All your days,
Until within your soul
  You know, and feel
His very Presence,
  The pinnacle of earthly bliss.

HE IS ABLE TO DO EXCEEDING ABUNDANTLY ABOVE ALL WE ASK OR THINK Ephes. 3 20

Expect the unexpected
From the Lord.
For He has promised in His Word
That He will do for you in love,
Exceeding abundantly above
All that you ask or think.

"But Lord, my mind is in such turmoil,
And I think and think so much,
That my thoughts are all entangled
For my needs are overwhelming,
And my hopes and fears are such
I cannot think aright to ask Thee
What I should."

"So, to Thee dear Lord, I cry;
For Thou knowest all my need,
And will all my wants supply
Before I ask.
Thus, upon Thy matchless wisdom,
In quiet resignation, I rely.
Do Thou all the choosing for me,
For I know, in perfect love
Thou wilt do for me far, far above
All that I could ask or think."

O LORD, HOW MANIFOLD ARE THY WORKS!
IN WISDOM HAST THOU MADE THEM ALL   Psalm 104   24

The swallows have come!
I have seen them,
On this lovely evening in May.
Come on a long, long journey
From lands far, far away.
Lands where the sun shines brightly
Day after day.
Now they are turning, soaring, swooping
In elegant display.

"Why little birds do you leave
Sunshine and cloudless skies;
Fly over the seas and hazard your lives,
Soar o'er the mountain where flies
The eagle, with glinting eyes searching
Landscape and sky
For frail little fliers like you?"

"How do your small bodies bear
With strong wind and driving rain?
Where do you rest and where feed?
And how do you find your way
To Britain's fair isles,
And your last nesting place
Under some old barn tiles?"

"Dear friend, if you carefully listen
The secret we'll twitter to you.
'Tis our Heavenly Father Who calls us
His will to do.
He planned it all, and He knows best
What is good for us — and you."

"O'er land and sea He guides us,
Ever sustains and for us provides.
And we have learned this lesson
Never His will to question.
In your ear the secret we'll whisper,
'Trust Him, and He'll see you through'."

ALL THINGS ARE POSSIBLE TO HIM THAT BELIEVETH
Mark 9 23

It is possible for you
  To take God's promises as true,
Trusting in them as they stand,
  Turning not to right or left hand.
Resting in His power to keep you
  And to give you VICTORY.

It is possible for you
  To cast upon Him every day
The trials and sorrows of your way,
  Because you know that He will share
The heavy burden which you bear
  And give you PEACE.

It is possible for you
  To have your mind kept true and pure
Lovely and free from sin's allure;
  Concentrating on the Saviour
In your speech and your behaviour
  Through FAITH in Him.

It is possible for you
  Quietly to accept His will,
Be it good or be it ill;
  To still quietly praise and pray
Through the darkness of the way
  By the Holy Spirit's POWER.

It is possible for you
  Throughout your journey here below,
The Presence of the Lord to know,
  Until that day, above the skies
You'll gaze upon Him with your eyes,
  Who for you did all things well.

THINE EYES SHALL SEE THE KING IN HIS BEAUTY

Isaiah 33 17

To meet on Earth is sweet,
  But when in Heaven we meet,
What everlasting joy 'twill be,
  For we shall be eternally
For ever with the Lord
  And one another.

And there, around His throne,
  With voices pure and clear,
From sinless hearts to Him we'll raise
  A song of everlasting praise,
That we are now made one with Him
  And one another.

With wonder we shall see
  The diadem adorn
His Kingly brow, where once was pressed
  The cruel crown of thorn.
Amazed upon Him we shall gaze
  And one another.

ENDURE HARDNESS AS A GOOD SOLDIER OF JESUS CHRIST *2 Timothy 2 3*

Stand up, be counted for Jesus
  If you love His Name.
'Though others may alter
  Do thou never falter,
Stand up, be counted for Him.

Stand up, be counted for Jesus,
  Stand up straight for Him;
Hide not your head in shame,
  Boldly declare His Name
Stand up, be counted for Him.

Stand up without shrinking for Jesus,
  Who bore in His body your sin
On Calvary's tree, rejected,
  Despised, scorned and neglected,
Stand up, be counted for Him.

Think of His spear-pierced side,
  Think of the crown of thorn,
Think of His sinless blood shed
  As He willingly died in your stead,
Stand up and be counted for Him.

Then one day He'll stand for you
  Before His Father's face,
And own your worthless name
  To all the blood-bought race
Who likewise owned His Name,
  Shrank not, despised the shame
Stood up and were counted for Him.

Then His voice of trumpet sound
  Through Heaven's vaults will resound,
"Well done, faithful soldier, well done,
  Receive the crown you have won
In Earth's evil sphere
  Where you showed no fear
To stand up, and be counted
FOR ME."

*JESUS SAYS, "COME UNTO ME
AND I WILL GIVE YOU REST"* *Matthew 11 28*

This book now ends,
But Oh! dear friends,
Have you seen the face of Jesus
In the pages?
Has His voice been calling to you
"Come unto ME and rest"?
If that is so, do not delay
Come to Him now – TODAY.
Come now. Come now
Before Him bow –
COME NOW.